BARCELONA CATHEDRAL

by
Canon J.M. Martí Bonet

with the co-operation of:
Ignasi Carbonell Gomis, Antoni Díaz Arnau,
Ramon Farrando and other members
of Barcelona Cathedral
of Volunteer Monitors.
Prologue by Monsignor Jaume Traserra.
Epilogue by Mn. J.M. Aragonès, canonge.

Photographs by Joan Cebollero

Layout and reproduction designed and produced by the technical services of
EDITORIAL ESCUDO DE ORO, S.A.,
Capítol Catedral and Arxiu Diocesà de Barcelona.
© Copyright of text and photographs of the current edition:
EDITORIAL ESCUDO DE ORO, S.A.

Editorial Escudo de Oro, S.A. and Arxiu Diocesà de Barcelona

LA SEU DE BARCELONA

Quan de sa immensa glòria
Catalunya es vegé en lo cimeral,
aprés d'haver collit en pau i en guerra
en tots lloredars de l'amplia terra
llorers de la victòria,
aixecar-ne volgué una catedral.
…
La nostra Seu
té la figura de Jesús en creu.
En lo creuer estesos
té sempre els amples braços,
frisós de veure'ns presos
amb tan dolcíssims i amorosos llaços.

Se cames són de naus:
l'acimbellada cúpula que espera
i sos dos campanars, que s'escamarlen
per dar pas a la gent, són les tres claus.
Lo chor és lo seu Cor, que d'amor bat
amb ritme harmoniós i acompassat;
extàtic prega i ora,
canta amb David i amb Jeremias plora.

Mn. Cinto Verdaguer

LIVING STONES

The prologue to this book is provided by an emotive poem by Monsignor Cinto Verdaguer. No better start could be provided for it. In it, the poet speaks of the period of maximum splendour and glory of Catalonia, when it was decided to build this Gothic Cathedral. In the early-14th century, people still remembered the «victory laurels» won by King James I and his grandson, James II. The great Catalan poet saw in Barcelona Cathedral the very figure of Christ on the cross. In those times, when Verdaguer was writing the poem, the famous dome had not been built, and for this reason he wrote that the «lofty dome... awaits» construction, which was not completed until 1916. It took over six centuries to finish the building of the Cathedral. The poet also affirms that «the choir (of the Cathedral) is its heart, with love beating in harmonious, rhythmic time; ecstatic, it prays, orates and sings». The poem takes on life anew when we visit it and pray in harmonious, rhythmic time in Barcelona Cathedral.

For many, going to Barcelona Cathedral is a veritable festivity: the people –lots of people– the Crist de Lepant, the Crypt of Santa Eulàlia, the colours of the stained-glass windows, the lamps, the grilles, the altarpieces, the organ, the Pieta by Bermejo, the Transfiguration by Bernat Martorell, the monstrance, the terrace roofs, the lantern, the cloister, the fountain with its geese... and, especially, the constant curiosity and manifest devotion embracing all those who enter it, are the elements which characterise this splendid monumental building and centre of worship in the heart of Barcelona's Gothic quarter.

Barcelona Cathedral is one of the city's historic monuments which attracts most visitors. It is estimated that over three million people immerse themselves in its marvellous enchantments every year. For this reason, and to help make visits even more rewarding, the Cultural Heritage Delegation of the Diocese of Barcelona has trained over one hundred volunteer monitors and guides who welcome and accompany all those who are interested in finding out more about the history of the religious and artistic treasure. We extend this welcome to all those visiting the Cathedral.

We hope, moreover, that this publication will form a friendly guide to all there is to be seen in the building, as well as a very personal souvenir of the visit, which has been organised with eight points for pause and historic, even catechistic, reflection. Through this, we trust that the «Cathedral of La Santa Creu i de Santa Eulàlia», to give the place its proud and glorious full name, will become, for all its visitors, a temple of living stones, for it speaks to us throughout of the meaning in the past of the guild spirit, of brotherhood, of solidarity, of the great charitable initiatives, such as the redemption of captives, the Pia Almoina, the hospitals, constant public and private prayer, sacred art and the authentic diocesan community. Barcelona Cathedral is the great symbol of its diocese and a constant stimulus to participate and emulate the most important moments in our history. In this way, we all become living stones forming part of the harmonious whole which is our Cathedral church.

Mons. Jaume Traserra
Bisbe auxiliar i president del
Capítol Catedral de Barcelona.

1. FROM THE PIA ALMOINA

The Pia Almoina is the registration and reception point for visitors to the Cathedral who wish to enjoy the explanations and descriptions of volunteers and monitors as they tour this monumental building, as well as the Diocesan Museum.

From the top floor of the Pia Almoina, with its splendid panoramic view of the Cathedral from the sculpture room with its long windows, one can appreciate:

* The importance of the canonry and the Pia Almoina from the point of view of *archaeology* (Roman tower and walls), *history* (Romanesque, Gothic and Renaissance elements, etc), *charity* (300 meals served to the poor every day), of the habitation of the *canons* (among them, Saint Oleguer) and reminders of the *Mercedarians* (Saint Peter Nolasco was probably buried here). Also pointed out is the building's other function, that of Diocesan Museum, where art exhibitions are also held.

* Outstanding is the statue of Saint Christopher (by Pere Gil and from the Church of Sant Miquel in Barcelona). This fine image symbolises the invitation to visit the Cathedral. The entrances of many cathedrals are adorned with the figure of this saint, in evocation of the legend according to which Christopher carried Christ across a river on his back. The statue, then, invites Christians to enter the Cathedral.

* Contemplating the building from the arches of the upper floor, we learn that three basilicas have existed over the course of 17 centuries: the *early Christian,* with its 4th-century baptistry; the *Romanesque* (11th century); and the present *Gothic* structure (begun at the end of the 13th century and completed as regards the main façade and dome, in 1913.

* The Cathedral is the symbol of the diocese, which has been graced by 119 bishops, from Pretextat (the first known) in 343 to the present Cardinal-Archbishop Ricard M. Carles. The Cathedral is considered the mother of all the churches in the archbishopric of Barcelona. It was dedicated to the Holy Cross and later, from the 9th century, shared this dedication with Eulàlia, patron saint of Barcelona. Since 599, moreover, and the Council of Barcelona in Visigoth times, it is denominated *sanctae crucis.* For this reason, the dome is crowned by the statue of Saint Helena, the mother of Constantine, who found the true cross of Christ. There is also a large cross on the Cathedral roof.

* We can here pause to describe the main features of the *façade.* It is the most recent element in the Cathedral, dating back to the late-19th and early-20th centuries. Its dome is 70 metres in height. In the chapter archives is a plan drawn on parchment by Carles Galtés de Ruán (known as Carlí) dating back to the year 1408, which formed part of the «Millenum» exhibition (1989) and in which we can clearly make out what was finally constructed by the architect Josep O. Mestre thanks to the patronage of Mr Girona and his children during the early-20th century. The façade consists of the portal and the dome, flanked by two towers, spires, statues of angels, saints and other Gothic-style ornamental elements. The portal is presided over by a large sculpture of Christ, surrounded by statues of the Apostles. Another outstanding feature are the stained-glass windows of the façade, many in Modernist style, though others are Renaissance. Particularly fine is the famous *Noli me tangere,* by glazier Gil Fontanet (1495), inspired by Bartomeu Bermejo, the artist responsible for the finest painting in the Cathedral: the *Pieta* (1490).

* Finally, we should mention the *external dimensions* of the Cathedral: it is 93 metres long, 40 wide and the nave reaches a height of 28 metres. The belltowers are 53 metres in height while, as we have already said, the dome has a height of 70 metres.

Saint Christopher, by Pere Gil, an alabaster sculpture from Sarreal (Tarragona province) dating back to 1545. There is a statue of this saint at the foot of most European cathedrals. In the figure of Christopher, who carried Jesus across the river, the Christian visitor sees an invitation to enter the church. The saint's name comes from the Latin «Christus» and the Greek «foros», meaning carrier of Christ, something all Christians must be.

Virgin of the hand-on-the-face in the Diocesan Museum of Barcelona. Polychrome alabaster. This is an early-14th-century statue found in the Church of the Mare de Déu de la Mercè. The Virgin is dressed in the garb of a Mercedarian. Some believe this statue to be the original image of La Mercè –Our Lady of Mercy– patron saint of the Archbishopric of Barcelona. A reproduction is installed in the Church of the Sant Patriarca Abraham in the Olympic Village. On the occasion of the 1992 Olympic Games, she was named «the Virgin of Welcome».

Main front of the Cathedral, completed in 1916 with the participation of sculptors from the Catalan Modernist movement. The hundred images of saints possibly refers to the Council of the One Hundred applied to the Church. The sculptors were: Rafael Atxé, P. Carbonell, E.B. Alentorn, A. Querol, F. Pagés i Senatossa, J. Roig i Soler and A. Vallmitjana.

The façade of the Cathedral, the Pia Almoina and the Casa de l'Ardiaca form the entrance into Barcelona's Gothic Quarter. On the left is the Mirador del Rei Martí and the belltower of Santa Àgueda.

The façade of the Cathedral in 1887 before the present front was built. The dome was covered by wooden coffering. Bottom left is the stained glass window known as «Noli me tangere».

When building the main front at the end of the 19th century, architect Josep Oriol Mestres bore in mind the design for the main doorway drawn up by the master Carlí (Carles Galtés de Ruan) in the year 1408.

The doorway in the main front is adorned by sculptures of angels, kings and prophets by Modernist sculptors Joan Roig and Agapito Vallmitjana, a total of 76 images, besides the twelve Apostles and the «Maiestas Domini».

A statue of Christ –known as «The Majesty of the Lord»– presides over the entrance to the Cathedral. It is the work of Agapito Vallmitjana. Behind are the wooden doors designed by Joan Roig.

Photo, above: Saint Peter and Saint Paul.

Below: statue of Saint James the Less, Saint Thomas, Saint Philip and Saint John.

Photo, above: Saint James the Great and Saint Matthew.

Below: statue of Saint Andrew, Saint Bartholomew, Saint Simon and Saint Judas (Tadeo).

Portal of saint Iu. The square and front are named after this saint due to the building opposite (now Tinell), for many years the domain of advocators and procurators, whose patron he is. Another theory makes saint Iu the patron saint of the builders of the front, who came from Flanders, his birth-place. The building at the side, now the F. Marés Museum, formerly housed the famed Barcelona Inquisition, and this institution's coat of arms is engraved on a stone here. The Portal of saint Iu is an early attempt at the lancet arch of Catalan Gothic architecture, which supports the great clocktower, proving that the pointed arch is just as dependable as the Romanesque semicircular arch. The belltower is 53 metres in height.

2. FROM THE GATE OF SANT IU

In the middle of Plaza de Sant Iu can be seen two large inscriptions on the jambs of the doorway. These tell us that the present Gothic Cathedral began to be built in 1298. The portal, in marble and stone from Montjuïc, has a structure typical of the early Gothic style, with elements recalling the Romanesque, particularly the bas-reliefs, and others taken from the previous basilica, such as a lion and a gryphon fighting with soldiers. The central tympanum features a statue of Saint Eulàlia, possibly from the school of Jaume Cascall. The niche is flanked by a number of orna-mental heads in bas-relief. In the arcades are the busts of angelic musicians, highly appropriate given the proximity of this portal to the organ. Also represented are staffs and other elements, originally installed to support statues now lost. Also interesting is the impressive pile of the clocktower and the entrance to the Chapel of El Rei Martí, from which the counts of Barcelona could attend religious ceremonies without needing to descend into the street, crossing a little bridge, now lost. This chapel was recently installed with a lift (3 May 1995). The construction of this portal was sponsored by builders from Flanders, where Saint Ivo was greatly venerated.

Impost representing a boot, installed in the outer wall (Carrer dels Comtes) indicating the Chapel of the Brotherhood of Saint Mark. At the beginning of the 15th century in Barcelona, furriers (who tanned and sold leather) and shoemakers alike were members of this brotherhood.

Stone bearing an inscription marking the commencement of the Gothic Cathedral during the time in office of Bishop Bernat Pelegrí (1298) under the reign of James II.

Statue of Saint Eulàlia of Barcelona with the palm of martyrdom and the Book of Acts of Saint Tirso. Attributed to the school of Jaume Cascall, late-14th century.

Imposts from the Romanesque Cathedral depicting the fight between a lion and a gryphon with soldiers. The construction of the Gothic Cathedral entailed the demolishment of the Romanesque basilica, though some of its sculptural elements were retained.

Entrance archway to the Chapel of El Rei Martí, a bridge from which communicated it with the Royal Palace, now the Palau del Lloctinent.

Belltower for the liturgical functions. Among the bells is the one known as Tomassa.

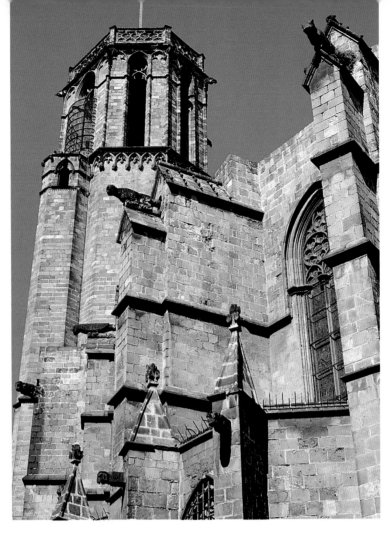

The gargoyles of Barcelona Cathedral are rightly famed. They are jutting channels which expel rainwater falling on the roof well away from the wall. They represent fantastic animals.

According to popular legend, these are witches and evil spirits who spat when the Corpus procession passed by. They were petrified into horrendous forms and condemned to spit out water from the roof when it rains.

Belltower containing the cathedral's largest bell, known as Eulàlia, which rings out the hours whilst Honorata chimes out the quarters. Nearby, a unicorn gargoyle.

Hebrew inscriptions taken from old tombs in Montjuïc Cemetery, now in the wall of the Palau del Lloctinent (formerly the Royal Palace).

Gargoyle representing an elephant.

3. FROM THE CATHEDRAL CHOIR

The Cathedral has a nave and two aisles, with apse, ambulatory and a sector resembling a crossing. There are four sections of nave, the largest at the foot of the Cathedral, as this has to support the dome. The typically Gothic buttresses give shape to the sixteen chapels opening up off the aisles. Each section has two chapels. At either end of the so-called *false crossing* are the two belltowers, dating back to 1386-1393, which can be climbed by two spiral staircases, each crowned by sculptures representing a snail.

From the choir can be seen the most important liturgical elements in the Cathedral: the cathedra, or bishop's throne, the altar, the cross to which the building is dedicated, the ambo and pulpit, the Crypt of Santa Eulàlia, the various assembly spaces, marked by voussoirs, the organ and, finally, the choir itself.

* *The cathedra.* The word «Cathedral» is derived from cathedra. The bishop's throne was carved in alabaster in the mid-14th century, its sculptor possibly the same as that responsible for the tomb of Saint Eulàlia. Over it was formerly the burial stone of a bishop, possibly Saint Oleguer, now in the sacristy of the Baptismal Chapel. The cathedra is of enormous importance, symbolising the power of the bishop and the faith of all the diocesans in the successor to the Apostles. A line of 119 bishops –all whose names are known– have successively sat in the cathedra of Barcelona Cathedral.

* *The altar.* The altar table presently rests on two large Visigoth capitals (6th century), though between 1939 and 1971 these were temporarily replaced by four small marble columns. However, in 1971, Canon Fàbrega had the original capitals restored to their rightful place. The altar is a fundamental element in the Cathedral, as it is a symbol of Christ and it is here that the Eucharist is celebrated.

* *The cross.* This presides over the upper space of the presbytery, and over the Cathedral itself. The cross is the work of Frederic Marés, cast in bronze and installed in 1976. The sculptural group represents the exaltation of the Holy Cross: Jesus Christ gloriously crowned on the crossed, surrounded by six angels.

Before 1971, the cross (now kept in the Sala de La Mercè) presided over the famous altarpiece, brought here in that year from the Church of Sant Jaume in Barcelona. The altarpiece was carved by an anonymous artist and later gilded. The lower section held the relics of Sant Sever (bishop of Barcelona, 633), which were brought here from Sant Cugat and transferred by Martí in 1405, according to the altarpiece in the Diocese Museum, the work of artists Pere Núnyes and Enric Fernández (1541).

* *Ambo and pulpit.* The ambo, from where the word of God is proclaimed, occupies a preeminent place in the presbytery. It was built in obedience to the Second Vatican Council in 1993. This ambo replaced the graceful pulpit in the choir, the work of the great Barcelonan sculptor Pere Ça Anglada (1403). This pulpit has a perfect hexagonal shape, the first section featuring a sculpture of the Virgin Mary with Baby Jesus (the Word made flesh) on her right arm and, on her left, the written Word.

In the lower section of the pulpit, forming brackets, are the figures of graceful flying angels, which crown magnificent ribbed decoration reminiscent of that of the nave. The pulpit is reached by a staircase carved in stone and sumptuously decorated by the sculptor Jordi Johan, who also completed the access jambs with two figures from the Annunciation, Mary and Gabriel. The door of this staircase is adorned by fine wrought iron work, whilst the bannister features a cresting of lilies. The sculptural group of the Virgin Mary and the Archangel Gabriel are now in the Cathedral Museum, and the staircase features copies by the cathedral's permanent sculptor, Barbero (1985).

* *The Crypt of Santa Eulàlia.* This is the most intimate corner in the Cathedral and the place where the most profound devotion to Barcelona's saint is expressed. The tomb was recently studied by historian J. Bracons who published his conclusion in the journal *D'Art* (1993) that it is the work of the Pisan sculptor Lupo di Francesco (1327). The crypt was built by Jaume Fabré, the first recorded architect in the construction of the Cathedral, during the pontificate of Bishop Ponç de Gualba (1303-1333). The crypt lies beneath the exact centre of the presbytery, under the high

altar, and is dedicated to the Mother of God. The entrance arch is almost flat, adorned with carved small heads, perhaps representing personages from the time of construction. In the centre of the arch is the head of a bishop, possibly Ponç de Gualba. The entrances to the two side chapels are crowned by two arches, decorated with carved human heads, on either side of the staircase. These chapels were walled off in 1779 when the crypt staircase was moved forward towards the high altar in order to increase the capacity of the Cathedral.

The crypt vault has two sections divided by twelve arches which converge into an enormous keystone in which are represented the Virgin Mary and Saint Eulàlia. The crypt is surrounded by a gallery (matroneum), in the centre of which stands a graceful alabaster sarcophagus carved by the sculptor Lupo di Francesco (1327), resting on eight columns, some fluted, others spiral, with Corinthian capitals and, in some cases, bases depicting human and animal figures. The walls of the sepulchre are decorated with magnificent haut reliefs depicting scenes from the martyrdom of Saint Eulàlia. On the front face of the tomb cover is represented the scene of the solemn transfer of the relics to this crypt and sarcophagus on 10 July 1339, a ceremony in which the papal legate was accompanied by monarchs, princes, noblemen and bishops. The rear face of the cover features a portrayal of the glorification of Saint Eulàlia, whilst the four upper angles of the tomb are adorned by attendant angels. In the centre, crowning the entire work, is the image of the Virgin Mary with the Child in Her arms. Set into the wall at the back of the crypt is the original tomb of Saint Eulàlia, dating back to the 9th century, and an authentic inscription commemorating the providential discovery of the remains of the saint in Santa Maria de las Arenas or Santa Maria del Mar (877).

Visitors will be greatly struck by the Cathedral choir, the backs of the stalls painted with 46 coats of arms by Joan de Borgonya. This commemorates the Chapter of the Order of the Golden Fleece, held in Barcelona in 1519 and presided over by Emperor Charles V. This meeting could well be seen as a precursor of what would now by the United Nations. Also of great interest are the misericords, or small seats, of the choirstalls, below which are sculptures of hunting scenes, games and other subjects not necessarily sacred.

The Chapel of Nostra Senyora de la Mercè is a highly representative baroque work. By an unknown artist, it dates back to around 1689 and represents the foundation of the Order of Our Lady of Mercy. This solemn act took place at the high altar of the Romanesque Cathedral itself on 10 August 1218 and the 775 anniversary was celebrated at a congress in 1993 attended by many Mercedarians, members of an order which does laudable charity work all around the world. The altarpiece represents Saint Peter Nolasco kneeling to receive the habit of the new order. Present at this ceremony were the young King James I, Berenguer de Palou and Saint Raymond of Peñafort. In the background is the Virgin Mary wearing the Mercedarian habit in evocation of the legend of her apparition. Two paintings dating back to 1688 depict Saint Peter and Pope Sylvester I, to whom this chapel was dedicated.

Above this «Chapel of the Souls» is the royal tribune, built for King Martin between 1407 and 1409. This area, as we have mentioned, was joined to the palace by a small bridge in the exterior, now lost.

Three essential elements of the Cathedral: the cathedra (origin of the word «Cathedral»), the Exaltation of the Holy Cross (which, with Eulàlia, gives the Cathedral its title); and the altar, supported by 6th-century Visigoth capitals.

The altar represents Christ Himself and is used to celebrate the Eucharist. According to the Second Vatican Council, the Church has always worshipped the Holy Scriptures and the body of Our Lord in a similar way, and has always taken from the table and shared amongst the faithful the Bread of Life, both of the Word of God and the Body of Christ.

The cathedra is the symbol of apostolic succession. We know the names of 119 bishops of Barcelona Cathedral. The back of the chair, carved during the pontificate of Cardinal Marcel Gonzàlez (1967-1972) rests on the 14th-century cathedra, attributed to the Pisan sculptor Lupo de Francesco. Over the cathedra is the coat of arms of the current Bishop Cardinal Ricard M. Carles.

Image of the Exaltation of the Holy Cross, by the artist Frederic Marés (1976). In the upper section is carved the keystone representing the crucifixion of Christ, with the symbolism of the Sun and the Moon, signifying light and darkness, resurrection and death.

The side walls of the stairs leading into the Crypt of Santa Eulàlia feature the heads of various dignitaries who patronised its construction.

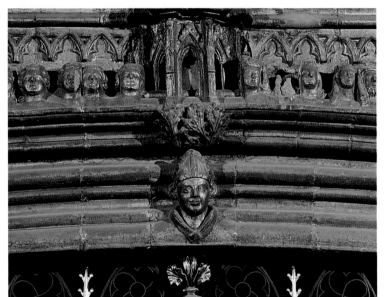

Head of Bishop Ponç de Gualba (1303-1334).

The ambulatory contains the most important stained-glass windows and Gothic chapels in the Cathedral.

Small keystone inside the crypt, depicting Saint Eulàlia.

Romanesque and Gothic sepultures of Saint Eulàlia.

Inscription commemorating the discovery of the relics of Saint Eulàlia in the Church of Santa Maria de les Arenes, or of El Mar in the year 877. The transcription translates as follows: «Here lies Saint Eulàlia, Christian martyr, who suffered, in the city of Barcelona, under the presidency of Daciano, the second day of the Ides of February and was found by Bishop Frodoí and his clergy in the Church of Santa Maria on (...) of the first of November. Thanks be to God.

Crypt of Santa Eulàlia in the chapel dedicated to the Virgin, which crowns the saint's sarcophagus. This is by the first architect of the Gothic Cathedral, Jaume Fabré, and to Pisan sculptor Lupo de Francesco (1327) during the pontificate of Bishop Ponç de Gualba.

Keystone in the crypt representing the Virgin with Baby Jesus, who caresses Saint Eulàlia, placing on her the martyr's diadem.

View of the Crypt of Santa Eulàlia with the magnificent tomb featuring scenes from the martyrdom of the saint and from the transfer of the relics to this crypt and sarcophagus on 10 July 1339. The sepulchre is crowned by an image of the Virgin with four candle-bearing angels.

Missal of Saint Eulàlia by Rafael Destorrents (1403), in the Barcelona Cathedral Archives. This page shows a representation of the Universal Judgement.

Complete view of the nave from the high altar (the nave's length, including the ambulatory and the presbytery, is 93 metres). At first, the access staircase began at the choir grille. In this way the canons, whilst praying in the choir, could see the tomb of Saint Eulàlia.

View of the throne and part of the choirstalls. The year 1519 saw the celebration of the 19th Chapter of the Order of the Knights of the Golden Fleece, dealing with European affairs including the possible Turkish invasion of Europe.

Panel in the throne by the sculptor Pere Ça Anglada (1403) representing the Virgin flanked by Saint Eulàlia and Saint Catherine. The image of the Virgin holds in her right arm the Baby Jesus (the Word made Flesh) and in her left the Bible (the Written Word).

The panel of the throne facing the bishop's seat in the choirstalls is a carving of Christ flanked by Saint Peter and Saint Paul. The third and fourth panels, not reproduced here, the feature Archangels Michael (with the scales), Raphael (with a fish) and Gabriel (with the Book of the Annunciation); and Saints and Deacons Lawrence, Stephen and Vincent.

The Cathedral choir. The stalls accommodated 200 canons who took part in the holy services every day. The number of canons varies according to the period. During the early days of the Gothic Cathedral there were 40, but this number later increased to include the Cathedral incumbents and incumbents of Saint Severe, who could attend services in the choir.

Below the pulpit are archings with keystones representing those of the Cathedral itself.

Six great artists took part in the construction of the Cathedral choir: Pere Ça Anglada (1394), Maties Bonafé with the collaboration of Antoni Claperós and John Lambert (1456) and Kassel and Michael Lochner (1499), responsible for the pinnacle-shaped baldachins.

Coats of arms of knights of the Order of the Golden Fleece; Charles I, Emperor Maximilian, Francois I of France and Henry VIII, King of England. Present knights of the Order include: Juan Carlos I, King of Spain, Philip, Prince of Asturias, Prince Charles, King Constantine II of Greece, King Charles XVI, Gustave of Sweden, Grand Duke John I of Luxembourg, Emperor Aki Hito of Japan, King Hussein of Jordan, Queen Beatrice of Holland, Queen Margaret II of Denmark, Elizabeth II of England, Albert II of Belgium and Harald V of Norway.

Misericord representing the killing of the pig.

At the ends of the rows of choirstalls are decorated wooden screens featuring scenes from the Passion and Resurrection of Christ. This one shows the descent of Christ in the place known as «Seol», where the righteous of the Old Testament awaited resurrection.

Misericord representing the game we now call hockey.

Misericord representing a dance scene.

The medallions of the choirstalls in many cases feature the figure of Christ, as all official prayer in the church takes place in the name of Jesus. For this reason such prayer pleases God; Christ Himself (Mystic Body) is who prays.

View of the nave and choir. In the centre, the sepulchral crypt containing the mortal remains of various canons. There were formerly installed in the choir two large lecterns with songsheets whose letter and music was large enough to be read from all chairs. Many of these songsheets are now kept in the Chapter Archives.

Sculptor Bartolomé Ordóñez of Burgos worked on the sculptures of the trascoro in around 1560. However, he was not able to complete it himself, and his pupil Pere Villar completed the work between 1563 and 1564, following the master's decorative design.

The scenes depicted in the trascoro represent scenes from the martyrdom of Saint Eulàlia. The niches contain statues of Saint Severe, Saint Oleguer, Saint Raymond of Penyafort and Saint Eulàlia, all linked to the story of the bishopric of Barcelona. From right to left the bas-reliefs are: Saint Eulàlia being judged by Daciano (sculpture by B. Ordóñez), flagellation (P. Villar), cremation (B. Ordóñez), crucifixion P. Villar).

The organ is often called the king of musical instruments. In the Cathedral, the organ accompanies divine service and prayers. Moreover, organ concerts are organised each month. The twills which formerly protected the organ pipes, decorated with grisailles, by Pere Serafí, are now kept in the Cathedral Museum. During the Napoleonic invasion, this was the last redoubt of the resistance in Barcelona. Three people hid in the bellows for several days, and the French troops were unable to find them until, finally, they gave themselves up.

* The organ. The organ is of great artistic and liturgical interest and importance. It underwent restoration from 1985 to 1994. It is housed below the belltower, in the upper gallery, under the Sant Iu Gate. It was built between the years 1537 and 1539. The great organ was formerly closed by twills decorated with grisailles by Pere Serafí, «the Greek». This artist, who also painted the great doors closing off the organ, was also known as *Pere de les set pes* («Pere of the Seven P's»), as there was a saying *Pere Pau pinta portes per poc preu* («Pere Pau paints doors for a low price»). He is thought to have carried out this work in around 1560. The twills were transferred to the Cathedral Museum in 1950. Concerts are now held almost every month, audiences filling the Cathedral and, needless to say, the organ also accompanies religious services held in the Cathedral. This, as we have said is, then, a very important organ. There are only four more of its class in Europe: those of the cathedrals of Saragossa, Daroca (Saragossa province), Palma de Mallorca and Perpignan.

Over all the years of its existence, the organ has undergone renovation on various occasions, for the most part needed due to lightning, even though there was a lightning conductor on the clocktower.

The first keyboard, or harmonium, the one nearest to the organist, is the oldest. The console was inside, facing the high altar. Now, after the latest restoration work, the organist plays the instrument with his back to the altar, so that the harmonium is behind him. It has 16 pedals and is manual. It plays the largest, fluted pipes, which are the original ones, dating back to the year 1540. The harmonium and registrations date back to the same period.

Since two years ago, the organ has had 61 registrations. The organist, memorising the combinations he chooses, can employ up to 96 possible combinations. The organ has four keyboards. It is said the third of these, the «expressive», or swell keyboard, is the most delicate because it is the highest placed and the keys are very long and any change of time can disorganise it. It is very rich in tonalities, with many more possibilities than the «great organ» (second keyboard) because it is possible to produce a huge variety of soft notes, whilst that of the great organ is a full sound. Then there is the fourth keyboard, which has two elements: the echo keyboard and that of battle. The echo keyboard has oboes, celeste... and are very soft, suited to late-19th century music, for the solos of Romanticism (the music of Mendelssohn, for example). The second keyboard, of that of battle, is a typically Spanish one with horizontal *trompetería.*

The pipes are made of tin, zinc, copper and lead. The sixteen feet are square and made from robust pinewood.

With such an old organ, one must speak of the bellowsmen, who worked huge bellows supplying the instrument with air. Nowadays, there are two soundless German engines to provide a uniform air supply, capable of ranging from pianissimo to fortissimo. The first engines caused such powerful vibrations that they had to be installed in a room adjoining the organ. In the space below the lift is the *Chapel of Les Ànimes del Purgatori,* formerly dedicated to the Holy Innocents as it was here that relics thought to belong to these martyrs were kept. The veneration of these relics gave rise to many popular traditions, such as the bisbetó, according to which on the Day of the Innocents, an altar boy dressed in bishop's attire would officiate ceremonies to the scandal of many of strict beliefs. References to this custom are found as early as the 14th century. The chapel was formerly installed with an arcosolium embedded into the wall containing the magnificent sarcophagus of Bishop Ramon d'Escales (1386-1398) by Antoni Canet (1409). Worthy of note are the crying figures under the Gothic arcades and the coat of arms of Bishop Escala, representing stairs.

Facing the organ on the side wall adjoining the sacristy are the tombs of Count Ramon Berenguer I, the Old, and his wife Almodís, founders of the Romanesque Cathedral (1046-1058). In 1545, the painter Enric Ferrandiz decorated the tombs, imitating a Renaissance architectural structure.

Typically Spanish horizontal trompeteria of the organ harmonium. Flanking the organ are statues of two angels with trumpets. Below was hung the traditional carassa –«large face»– now in the Cathedral triforium. The mouth of the carassa opened when the organist played a deeper note or on certain days when sweets would be thrown out from it. Under the organ, the vault of the Entrance of Sant Iu also features magnificent keystones representing Saint Peter.

4. FROM THE ROOFS

Magnificent panoramic views of the city and of the Cathedral itself can be enjoyed from the cross which presides over the exterior part of the nave, or from the dome. From here, we can see all the great landmarks of the city: La Mercè, Columbus, the shipyards, Santa Maria del Pi, Sant Agustí, Montjuïc, the Sagrada Familia, the Palace of Justice, the Mirador del Rei Martí, El Tinell, Santa Àgueda, Santa Maria del Mar, the Olympic Village, Sants Just y Pastor, the City Hall, the Palace of the Generalitat, Sant Severe, Sant Felip Neri, the Episcopal Palace, the Casa de l'Ardiaca, the Pia Almoina, etc.

Here the visitor should also pause to examine the architectural structure of the Cathedral, with its nave and two aisles (buttresses and flying buttresses) and the two belltowers. These towers (53 metres in height) correspond one the one hand, to the civil belltower (clocktower) and, on the other, to the ecclesiastical. They are perfectly octagonal in shape, with an adjoining prismatic body (crowned by a carved snail) for the staircase. The belltowers were built between 1386 and 1393.

The life of city and of the Cathedral itself went on to the rhythm of the bells, which were baptised and received names. The largest in the clocktower, weighing 3 tonnes is called Eulàlia, whilst over it is Honorata. In the ecclesiastical belltower are, from top to bottom, Dolors, Severa, Angèlica, Antònia, Oleguera, Gregòria, Narcisa, Mercè and the famous Tomassa. The bells ring out to call worshippers to the religious services, their pealing and tolling singing out, rejoicing, mourning and announcing prayers in church. Historically, the bells were rung to announce a series of events: the Angelus (at eight o'clock in the morning, twelve noon and seven in the evening); the «toc del rei» (at two in the afternoon, calling worshippers to pray for the Cathedral benefactors, particularly the king); the «toc del seny del lladre» which rang out at night to announce the closing of the gates in the city walls, warning of thieves; and the ringing out of each liturgical office: matins, lauds, prime, tertia, sext, nones, vespers and compline.

The «Salomons», or skylights, on all the roofs serve to ventilate the interior of the Cathedral or as supports for the lighting fixtures. Many of the sculptural groups adjoining the towers and the dome can also be seen on the roofs (Saint George, Saint Eulàlia, the Cathedral cross, that of Saint Eulàlia, the cat and the mice, the eagle...).

The Cathedral roof features corbels, cornices, spires and gargoyles decorated with a variety of decorative motifs: the miser, Saint George with the damsel and the dragon, exotic birds, etc.

In their free time, the bellringers used to play different games, such as the one depicted on the stone on one side of the dome. This game is known today as «molinet» («little mill»), already popular in Roman and medieval times, as the photograph shows.

The Cathedral dome is one of the monument's most outstanding elements It is crowned by a statue representing Saint Helena, mother of Constantine, thanks to whom the true cross of Christ was found in Palestine. Coincidentally, Helena was also the name of the mother of Manuel Girona, the great Maecenas of the main façade of the Cathedral. The sculpture of Saint Helena is by Eduard Batiste Alentorn (1856-1920). It has been possible to go up to the dome since 1995, enabling visitors to enjoy a marvellous panoramic view of the city between its arches and balustrades.

The cresting of the dome is adorned with statues of winged angels.

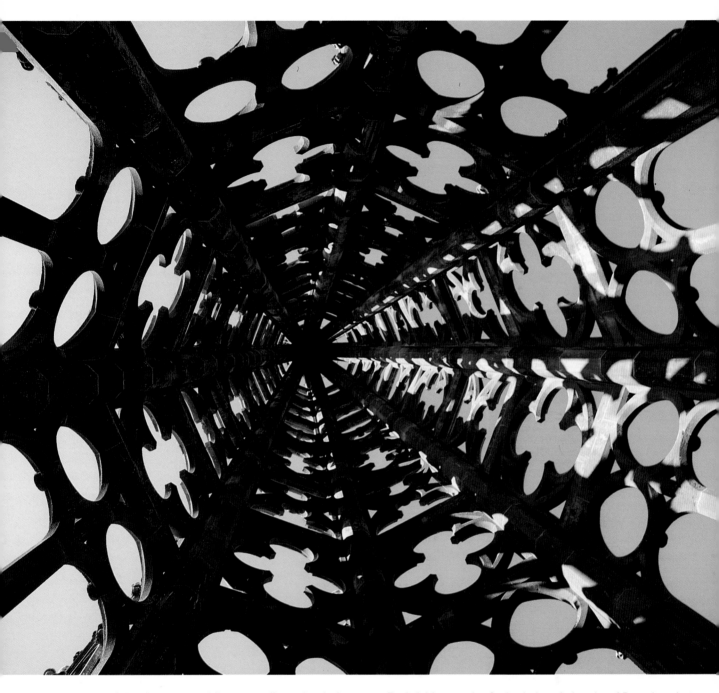

Interior of the dome, resembling a peculiar stained-glass window in which the glass is replaced by sky blue or grey cloud. Some also liken it to a work of embroidery or crochet, or a simple paper cut-out, but all agree that this is a splendid example of Modernist architecture.

Each 3 May, on the Cathedral roof, the city of Barcelona is blessed in the four cardinal points. The cross is situated directly above the presbytery. Legend has it that on this same spot, when Saint James ended his preaching, he took two pine branches and formed the shape of the cross with them.

From high up in the dome, visitors are treated to one of the finest views over Barcelona between arches, spires, belfries and graceful angels which appear ready to take to the air in defence of the city: these are the messengers of the sky, serene, peaceful, delicate and charming.

From inside the dome, one can look down at the nave and the magnificent keystone representing Christ in His glory, surrounded by angels. To one side is the coat of arms, featuring a pear, of the patriarch Sapera, bishop of Barcelona from 1410 to 1430. The keystones remind us of Jesus' words: «the stone the builders rejected is now the cornerstone» (Matthew 21, 42). They are the guarantee that the arches, the entire monument, will not come crashing down. For this reason, they are viewed with admiration and commiseration. They are imbued with enormous symbolism, indicating the liturgical functions which take place below or the original functions (charities, guilds, altarpieces, etc) of their chapels. The keystone next to the dome of the nave reminds us that we are in the house of Christ, who welcomes us.

5. FROM THE GALLERY

Going down the stairs of the left-hand tower, next to the dome, we come to the U-shaped gallery over the side chapels. This is now used to house the neo-Gothic monument dating back to the late-19th century which was used on Easter Thursday and Good Friday as the reserve of the holy of holies. The wings of the gallery now also contain various archive offices, that of the chapter secretariat and other dependencies devoted to the restoration and conservation of the altar-pieces and works of art. There is also a fine collection of ceramics and, to the left, the old rooms of the famous Chapter Archives. Also displayed are the gargoyle and the parchment document by which the industrialist Girona donated half a million pesetas to enable the façade to be completed, as well as two models showing how the Cathedral would have looked without the choir in the middle.

Over the gallery and the radial chapels of the ambulatory, surrounding the entire nave, is a false triforium which allows a view of the vault keystones from a distance of about three metres.

The stained-glass windows can also be contemplated here from close at hand, particularly the Gothic windows in the ambulatory, featuring the coats of arms of bishops Ponç de Gualba, Arnau de Gurb, Sapera, etc.

At this point, the visitor also has the chance to see the importance of the chapter archives, which researchers reach by the lift from the Chapel of Santa Lucía. The archives contain various papyrus documents dating to the 5th-8th centuries, some 200 codices (including a number of magnificent miniatures such as the Santa Eulàlia d'en Destorrents prayer book), around one hundred incunabula, over 40,000 parchments (9th-17th centuries) and the records of many archive series, such as the Mensa Capitular and the Pia Almoina. These archives, we must remember, represent the memory of our Cathedral church and the written record of the faith of our ancestors. The contain the life –with all its good deeds and its mistakes– of the chapter institutions and of the faithful who partook of the charitable actions of the Cathedral.

At the top of the nave, bordering it, is a triforium or gallery. During restoration work in 1970, the polychrome of the keystones, which had become blackened over the centuries, was discovered.

20th-century stained-glass windows in the triforium, at the foot of the Cathedral. In the first is Saint James the Great, Saint Anthony Abad, Saint Alexander and Saint Joaquima Vedruna; in the second, Saint Severe, Saint Joseph Oriol, Saint Medir and Saint Vincent Ferrer. The first was sponsored by Barcelona Provincial Government, the second by Barcelona City Council.

Stained-glass window of the porch of the main front.

Stained-glass window of La Creu Santa i Santa Eulàlia. Royal coats of arms and coats of arms, probably of Bishop Ponç de Gualba. 14th century.

Stained-glass window of Sant Silvestre. The figure of the pope is flanked by the heads of saints (bishops, cardinals, ...). 15th century.

Stained-glass window of Sant Andreu. The saint wears the cross around his neck. The coats of arms, one on each lance, pertain to Bishop Armengol, dating the window to 1398-1408. The traceries features: a sun and a moon (below) and the royal coat of arms (above).

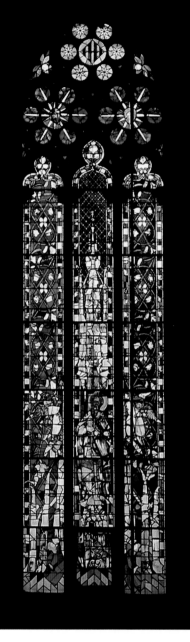

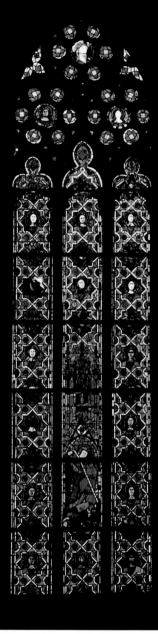

Stained-glass window of Sant Esteve. The saint holds the palm of martyrdom in his right hand and a chalice in his left. Over the small baldachin, a Christ in one border shows the wound in His right hand, whilst he holds a book in His left.

Stained-glass window of Sant Antoni Abat, by Nicolau de Maraya, 1405-1407.

Stained-glass window of Sant Miquel Arcàngel. In his right hand, Michael holds a spear, with which he kills a kind of serpent wound around his feet. 14th-15th centuries.

Our Lady of El Bust and Saint Gregory Taumaturg flanked by angels, along with the coat of arms of Dr Gregori Modrego, Archbishop of Barcelona (1942-1967).

Our Lady of the Angels and Saint Bartholomew Apostle, flanked by angels. Stained-glass window donated by Bartomeu Barba, Governor of Barcelona. A. Oriach, 1946.

Stained-glass window of La Puríssima Concepció and of San Francesc de Borja. 20th century.

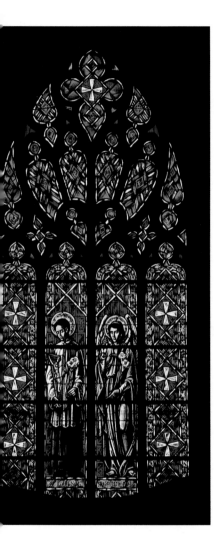

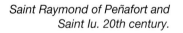

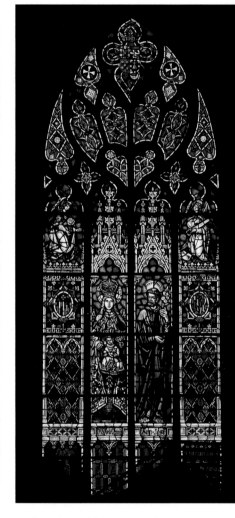

Stained-glass window of Sant Lluís Gonzaga i de l'Arcàngel Sant Gabriel. 20th century.

Saint Raymond of Peñafort and Saint Iu. 20th century.

Our Lady of Mercy and Saint Joseph with Mercedarian escutcheons and the anagram of Saint Joseph. 20th century.

Barcelona Cathedral has 215 keystones. Those of the nave are as follows:

Over the high altar, where the Eucharist is celebrated, the crucifixion of Christ flanked by two figures: on the right, the Virgin, and on the left, Saint John. The upper section features the moon and the sun.

Saint Eulàlia, over her crypt. Beside her is the coat of arms of Queen Blanche of Anjou, in a starry background.

The Virgin of Misericord, her cloak open to contain, on the left, the pope, the king, a cardinal, a bishop and a canon, and on the left the queen, a nun and three unidentified figures. This keystone dates back to the year 1379.

Annunciation of the Virgin by the Archangel Gabriel. In the centre is a jar with lilies symbolising purity and, above, the Holy Spirit descending over the Virgin, who holds in her hand an open book. Keystone (1379).

Bishop in pontifical robes with deacons. The deacon on the right holds the Bible, the deacon on the right the crozier. The coat of arms is that of Bishop Pere Planella (1371-1385).

Christ in His glory surrounded by angels holding the world with the cross in His left hand, whilst He blesses it with His right. The work is by the sculptor Pere Joan (1418) and was installed in the time of the bishop and patriarch Francesc Climent Sapera.

Close to the door in Plaça de Sant Iu is a keystone representing Saint Peter seated on his cathedra. He is surrounded by four more smaller keystones, trefoiled and also polychrome.

Keystone over the main entrance representing the resurrection of Christ, who walks out of the tomb whilst the soldiers sleep on the ground.

Keystone representing Saint John with the eagle, seated at the escritorium with an inscription from the beginning of his Gospel, reading «In the beginning...». It is situated in the false transept over the cloister door and is surrounded by four other keystones featuring decorative motifs.

Modernist stained-glass window representing the scene with Mary Magdalene and Christ resuscitated («Noli me tangere»). Drawing by Bermejo and by Gil Fontanet.

Tomb of Bishop Ramon d'Escales by the sculptor Antoni Canet (1409).

Predella of the Altarpiece of the Archangel Gabriel, by the painter Lluís Barrassà (1381-1390), representing the Birth of Our Lord, the Virgin seated on the «Sedes Sapientiae» and the Epiphany.

6. FROM THE AMBULATORY

It was precisely at the ambulatory that the Gothic Cathedral began to be built, almost 700 years ago. We know that the work began on 1 May 12948 during the period in office of Bishop Bernat Pelegrí and under the reign of James II, and that they were terminated, practically, during the times of Bishop-Patriarch Climent Sapera during the reign of Alphonse V of Aragon. We are told, too, by the books of records, that the old Romanesque basilica was taken down –probably with little concern to save the objects of art it contained– as the Gothic edifice was built. Except for the dome and the façade, the Gothic cathedral was completed over 150 years, and we can divide this period into three stages.

During the first, the entire building was planned and construction began of the apse with its radial chapels, the presbytery with its high altar and crypt, and the false crossing. During this period, the work was directed by Jaume Fabré, and there exist many records of the contribution made by the faithful and the clergy. Bishop Ponç de Gualba (1303-1334) is often recorded as commuting sentences of excommunication to fines which went towards the building of the Cathedral.

The second stage saw the extension of the nave and aisles with their side chapels up to the height of the trascoro.

During the third, executed thanks, fundamentally, to the patriarch Sapera (d. 1430), the lower section of the dome was built and covered with wood coffering and the chapels at the foot of the church were opened through the construction of wider arches. In 1417, the Cathedral was closed by a simple wall until such time as the façade should be built. This was designed by Carles Galtés de Ruán, «Carlí», on 27 April 1408 according to the parchment now kept in the Sala de la Traça. Carlí drew 111 figures besides the central figure, which represented the *Maiestas Domini*.

The ambulatory has ten radial chapels, of which we have already described the first and the third (from left to right). Between that of Les Ànimes and that of La Mercè is the chapel recently dedicated to the Holy Heart, containing a sculpture by Vicenç Vilarrubias (1940).

The fourth chapel is that of *Santa Clara y Santa Catalina d'Alexandria.* The altarpiece is by Miquel Nadal and García de Benavarri (1456) and was paid for by Sança Ximenis de Cabrera, who wished to be buried here, though his mausoleum was finally built in the Chapel of Sant Cosme y Sant Damià. The walls of the Chapel of Santa Clara y Santa Catalina are adorned with paintings depicting scenes of the martyrdom of Saint Stephen, patron saint of the Barcelona harness-makers' guild, to which this chapel formerly pertained.

The fifth chapel is dedicated to Saint Peter, though the altarpiece, by Joan Matas of Girona (1415), is of Saint Martin of Tours and Saint Ambrose. The side walls feature two paintings of scenes from the life of Saint Peter.

The sixth chapel is that of *Santa Helena,* but the altarpiece is of the Archangel Gabriel, an anonymous work dating back to the period 1381-1390. Up until the year 1932, this altarpiece was kept in the cloister and the statue of the Christ of Lepanto was venerated in this chapel.

The seventh chapel is that of Saint John the Baptist *(Capella de Sant Joan Baptista)* and features an altarpiece by an anonymous artist depicting scenes from the life of the saint, dating back to the year 1577. The chapel is now dedicated to Saint Joseph, patron saint of the guild and brotherhood of master carpenters. A statue of Joseph is installed in the 18th-century tabernacle. The side walls have two fine doors by Joan Matas of Girona (1415).

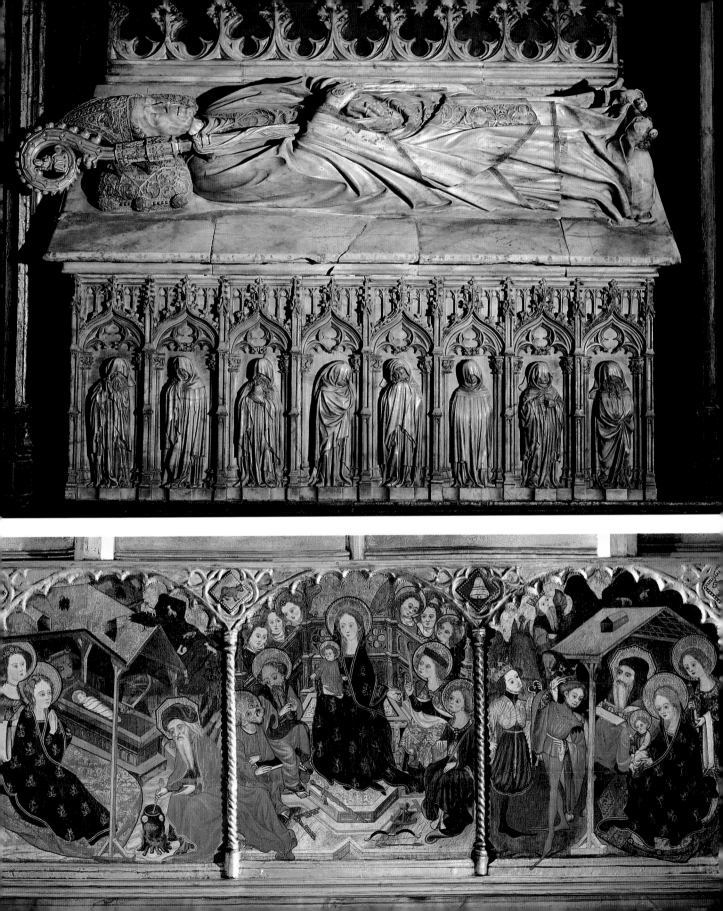

The eighth chapel features the famous altarpiece of the *Transfiguration of the Lord,* recently restored by the Monastery of Sant Cugat Restoration Centre, by Bernat Martorell (1450). This altarpiece was paid for by Bishop Simó Salvador (d. 1445). Also in this chapel, on the left-hand wall inside an arcosolium, is the mausoleum of Bishop Ponç de Gualba (1303-1334), so often mentioned in this guide. The mausoleum, or at least the calvary crowning it, is by Jaume Cascall.

In the ninth chapel is the altarpiece of the *Visitation of Mary,* by an anonymous artist (1466-1475). Its painting was commissioned by Canon Nadal Garcès, who is depicted at the foot of the altarpiece. On the left is the mausoleum of Bishop Berenguer de Palou (1212-1241), who received votes of redemption from captives of the first Mercedarians. This possibly formed part of one of the Romanesque chapels before the construction of the Gothic Cathedral.

In the tenth and last chapel is a baroque altarpiece dating back to the year 1712 and dedicated to *Saint Anthony Abad.* This chapel formerly pertained to the muleteers' guild.

Next, we come to the sacristy, where we can see the Cathedral treasure. The wall near the entrance features decorative stone crenellated elements crowned by a very tall cross. To one side were installed in 1545 the tombs of Ramon Berenguer and Almodis, count and countess of Barcelona and founders of the second Cathedral, dating back to 1046-1058. These are wooden coffins covered in scarlet velvet, installed in the wall over a painted background imitating an architectural structure, by the painter Enric Ferrandis (1545).

In the sacristy are two Romanesque high windows from the earlier Cathedral. In 1408 and again in 1502, this dependency was extended with the construction of the little room for the treasure and then the room now used by the priests to put on their vestments.

The **treasure** contains Barcelona cathedral's famous monstrance, in gold and silver plating, wrought metal elements and encrusted jewels. Inside the tower-shaped ostensorium, the vault key is of enamel encrusted in gold. Though no buril has been found, this is a work made in Barcelona during the late-14th century, between 1370 and 1390. It has three sections: the seat supporting the hexagonal tower showing the Holy Form, and the two crowns. According to a legend recorded in the sacristy accounts as far back as 1492, the seat was given to the Cathedral by King Martin (1396-1410). Nevertheless, we know that Barcelona was one of the first cities of the Christian world where Corpus Christi was celebrated with a procession, a tradition which began here in 1320, when the city councillors donated a silver-plated monstrance encrusted with precious stones to the Cathedral, though this was returned in 1370. The present monstrance has been much studied, particularly on the occasion of three great exhibitions: «Thesaurus» (1986), «Millenum» (1989) and «Catalunya Medieval» (1992).

The second most valuable item in the Cathedral collection of silverwork is the processional cross by Francesc Vilardell (1383). This is silver plated with fleur-de-lys at the ends and the images of the crucifix and Saint Eulàlia on either side with two lovely translucent enamels.

Besides these two outstanding items, the treasure also contains two 11th-century *lipsanotecas,* Saint Oleguers' mitre (12th century), Arnau de Gurb's crozier (13th), a small Moorish ivory chest (13th), a small polychrome alabaster altarpiece of Our Lady of the Rosary (14th), the small chest of Saint Severe (15th), the Lignum crucis (14th), the sword of High Constable Pedro of Portugal, who reigned in Catalonia as Pere IV, (1460), a statue of Saint Eulàlia by Joan Perutxena (1644) and a statue of the Child Jesus by Ramon Amadeu (d. 1821), amongst others.

Altarpiece of the Transfiguration, by the master Bernat Martorell (1445-1452), representing Jesus and the Woman of Samaria, and a fragment from the Descent from the Cross.

Altarpiece of the Transfiguration, by the master Bernat Martorell (1445-1452), representing the healing of the possessed.

Fragment from the Altarpiece of the Transfiguration, by the master Bernat Martorell (1445-1452), representing the Wedding at Canà.

Fragment from the Altarpiece of the Transfiguration, by the master Bernat Martorell (1445-1452), representing the Miracle of the bread and the fishes.

Fragment from the Altarpiece of the Transfiguration, by the master Bernat Martorell (1445-1452), representing the Jesus talking with Moses and Elijah and, below, Saint Peter, Saint John and Saint Andrew.

A gold, enamelled keystone figures adorns the monstrance in the Custodia, or Cathedral treasure.

(Photograph by Miquel Serra).

Barcelona Cathedral's Custodia: royal crowns, a monstrance surrounded by a royal chain and the throne of King Martin. Local Barcelona work between 1370 and 1390.

In the Custodia, particularly in the ostensory, everywhere, in mouldings, windows, gargoyles, are jewels in the form of figures or precious stones. Among them is a jewel representing a cockerel and another depicting Christ resuscitated, leaving the tomb.

According to legend, the throne was donated by King Martin (1396-1410). Its frame is covered by an enamelled ornament, probably from Naples.

The monstrance, which contains a rich and valuable, jewel-encrusted viril, or smaller monstrance, represents the architectural elements of a Cathedral.

Some of the bishops of Barcelona bequeathed their pastoral rings to the Custodia, and the Cathedral treasure features those of Cardinal Casañas and Archbishop Gregori Modrego, among others.

Two crowns, said by some to have been donated by Queen Violant, third wife of John I, and by others to have been a gift of King Martin.

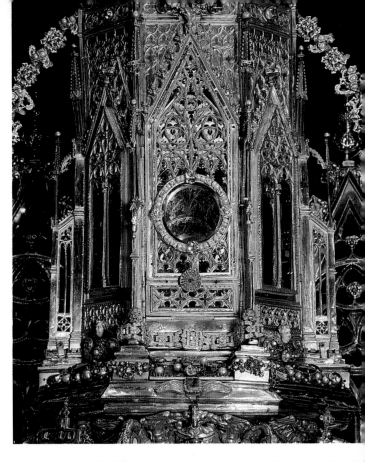

Processional cross of Santa Eulàlia by the silversmith Francesc Vilardell (1383). It features splendid enamels representing the four Evangelists, the Last Dinner, the Marys, Saint John and the soldiers, the pelican, Adam leaving the tomb.

Mitre of Saint Oleguer, Bishop of Barcelona and Archbishop of Tarragon from 1115 to 1137 (seen here from the front and from behind).

Crozier of Arnau de Gurb, Bishop of Barcelona from 1252 to 1284.

Casket of Saint Severe, with ivory encrustations representing scenes from his life. The relics were solemnly transferred from Sant Cugat to Barcelona in 1414.

Mitre of Bishop Urquinaona (1878-1883).

Sword of Condestable (15th century).

The Vera Creu, or True Cross (15th century).

The small Altarpiece of La Mare de Déu del Roser, by an anonymous Italian artist in the 15th century. Made from ivory, it represents the Mysteries of the Rosary.

Statue of Saint Eulàlia by the silversmith Joan Perutxena (1644). In a cabinet in the Cathedral treasure are baroque croziers and mitres, chalices, ciboriums, reliquaries and, at the foot, the 13th-century crozier of Arnau de Gurb.

Carved polychrome sculpture of Baby Jesus, by Ramon Amadeu. Late-18th century.

17th-century gilt chalice, encrusted with ivory.

The outer wall of the choir features representations of Biblical personages: in these two photographs, Moses and Isaiah. Probably the work of Antoni Claperós.

Until 1970, the carassa, or large face, was situated under the organ, but it has since been installed in the triforium. It was a tradition on the Feast of the Holy Innocents for these carassas to open their mouths during matins and to throw out sweets and pastries for the children.

Ornamentation of the entrance to the sacristy.

7. FROM THE CHAPELS TO THE AISLES

The aisles have a total of nine chapels, not counting the ten of the ambulatory. Leaving the sacristy and passing the false crossing, from left to right, we come first to the *Chapel of Sant Pacià.* The altarpiece, restored in 1994, is baroque, the work of Miquel Sala (1688). Over the altar steps is a reclining statue of Saint Francis Xavier. This is a truly magnificent altarpiece depicting scenes from the life of the saint, bishop of Barcelona (died in around 395) and medallions with scenes from the life of Christ. On the floor of this chapel is the tomb of Bishop Joan Dimas Loris (d. 1598), a great promoter of devotion towards the saintly Bishop Pacià.

The *Chapel of Nostra Senyora del Pilar.* This has a 16th-century baroque altarpiece featuring images of Our Lady of the Pillar, Saint Barbara and Saint Tecla. The chapel also contains the tomb of the first archbishop of Barcelona, Gregori Modrego by sculptor Frederic Marés (1972).

The *Chapel of Sant Pau i Sant Gaietà.* The altarpiece in this chapel is attributed to Domènech Talarn (1902).

The *Chapel of Sant Ramon de Penyafort.* The saint to whom this chapel is devoted is closely linked to the Cathedral. He was a «mestre», master, though no records that he ever became a canon have been found. Nevertheless, he was one of the church leaders in the 13th century. His tomb was transferred here from the Convent of Santa Catalina after the disentailment of 1835. Dating to the 14th century, it features representations of scenes from the life of the saint. Under the altar is the burial stone bearing a bas relief of the saint.

The *Chapel of Sant Pancraç.* This saint enjoys great popular devotion. The chapel contains a baroque gilt polychrome altar dating to the 18th century.

The *Chapel of Sant Josep Oriol.* The altar is Modernist in style. In the left-hand wall is the tomb of Cardinal Salvador Casañas (d. 1908), who promoted the canonisation of Barcelonan Saint Josep Oriol (1650-1702). Pope Pious X declared him a saint in the year 1909.

The *Chapel of Sant Cosme y Sant Damià.* The altarpiece is by Bernat Martorell, who personally painted the *Transfiguration.* In the left-hand wall is the tomb of Sança Ximenis de Cabrera, carved in alabaster by Pere Oller (1436). Above is a painting attributed to Lluís Dalmau (1460).

The *Chapel of El Sant Crist de Lepant y de Sant Oleguer.* It should be remembered that the interior of this space was formerly the chapterhouse, and that in the part giving onto the aisle were two chapels. Saint Oleguer was canonised in 1676, and for this reason the chapterhouse, built by Arnau Bargués in 1407, was converted into the bishop's mausoleum. The reclining statue of Saint Oleguer is by Pere Ça Anglada (1406). The funeral urn is baroque in style, and by Francesc Grau and Domènech Rovira in the 17th century. Passing the altar on either side, we come to a small chamber, richly decorated with jasper and marble, carved doors and coffering with painted panels, attributed to Antoni Viladomat or, perhaps, Manuel Tramulles. In the centre of this chamber lie the mortal remains of the saint,

one of the most eminent bishops of medieval Europe. Saint Oleguer was born in Barcelona and was a canon and prepositus of the Cathedral, abbot of Sant Ruf of Avignon and bishop of the city by imposition of the pope. He was adviser to counts Ramon Berenguer III and IV, legate to Pope Paschal II and archbishop of Tarragona. He died, considered a great saint, in 1137. Over the Mausoleum of Sant Oleguer is the crucifix of the Christ of Lepanto, dating back to the 16th century and which, according to tradition, presided over the flagship of the Christian fleet commanded by John of Austria which sank the Turkish fleet in the Gulf of Lepanto during the papacy of Pious V (1571). The keystone of the central vault in the chapterhouse is by Joan Claperós in 1454 and represents the Feast of Pentecost. In the central floor of the chapel is the tomb of Bishop Manuel Irurita.

At the foot of the Cathedral are two chapels: the first on the right, adjoining the Chapel of El Sant Crist de Lepant, is the *Chapel of La Immaculada.* The statue is recent and depicts the Virgin holding the keys of the city, offered to Her by the city council as an ex-voto offering during the plague of 1651. In the left-hand wall is the tomb of the patriarch (of Jerusalem) and bishop of Barcelona Francesc Climent Sapera (1430). The mausoleum dates back to the year 1899.

The chapel on the left-hand side is the *Chapel of El Baptisteri.* It is situated very close to the baptistry of the early Christian church in the subsoil. The font is made from Carrara marble, carved into the form of a cup with helicoidal edges, by the Florentine artist Onofre Julià (1433). Also interesting is the stained-glass window *(Noli me tangere)* by Gil Fontanet, inspired by the great artist Bartomeu Bermejo, a native

of Córdoba but who resided in Barcelona for several years at the end of the 15th century and who is the artist responsible for the finest painting in the Cathedral: the *Pieta* (1490).

The *Chapel of Sant Sever* contains an altarpiece by the Barcelonan sculptor Francesc de Santa Creu (1683). The *Chapel of Sant Marc* has a baroque altarpiece – restored along with that in the previous chapel over the 1992-93 period– built and decorated from 1683 to 1692 by an anonymous artist. On either side are paintings by Francesc Tramulles (1763). The is the chapel pertaining to the guild of master shoemakers. In the *Chapel of Sant Bernardí* –which pertains to the matt-maker's guild– is a simple altarpiece dating back to 1705 and containing three images: Saint Bernard, Saint Michael and Saint Anthony of Padua.

The *Chapel of La Mare de Déu del Rosari* has a lovely altarpiece, the work of Agustí Pujol, an artist from nearby Terrassa (1619). This is an early Catalan baroque work. The chapel also contains the burial stone of Canon Guillem (13th century).

The next chapel features an altarpiece dedicated to Saint Bartholomew and Saint Elizabeth, by the painter Guerau Gener (1401), a follower of Lluís Borrassà. In the floor is the tomb of Barcelonan Auxiliary Bishop Ricard Cortés, who died in 1910.

The *Chapel of Sant Sebastià i Santa Tecla* has an altarpiece by Rafael Vergós and Pere Alemany (1486-1498).

The *Chapel of La Mare de Déu de l'Alegria* and the *Chapel of Montserrat* both contain altarpieces dating to this present century. The statue in the first is by the sculptor Camps i Arnau (1945), whilst the paintings in the second date to 1940.

Prior to the 20th century, the Chapel of the Santíssim was the same as that of Sant Joan Evangelista in the Cathedral ambulatory. At the beginning of this century it was transferred to the present Chapel of El Crist de Lepant i de Sant Oleguer. At the foot of the Altar of El Santíssim is the tomb of the bishop and martyr Dr. Manuel Irurita, died in 1936.

Sagrary by the silversmith Corberó. Enamels by the Escola Massana. Barcelona, 1965.

Behind the Chapel of El Santíssim is the uncorrupted body of Saint Oleguer, bishop of Barcelona and Archbishop of Tarragona (1115-1137). This tiny space also contains paintings by Viladomat (1780).

Baroque Altarpiece of Sant Pacià, by artist Miquel Sala (1688). The scene under the niche represents the Last Supper, in which the artist places Saint Ignatius with the rule of the Company of Jesus.

There is a statue of the saint below the Altar of Sant Ramon de Penyafort. The sarcophagus and relics were originally in the former Convent of Santa Caterina dels Dominics de Barcelona, now lost.

Chapel of La Puríssima. The Virgin holds the keys to Barcelona. The statue is a recent polychrome carving.

Tomb of Sança Ximenis of Cabrera, with a painting attributed to Lluís Dalmau (1460).

Mausoleum of Cardinal Casañas (died 1908) by the sculptor Josep Llimona.

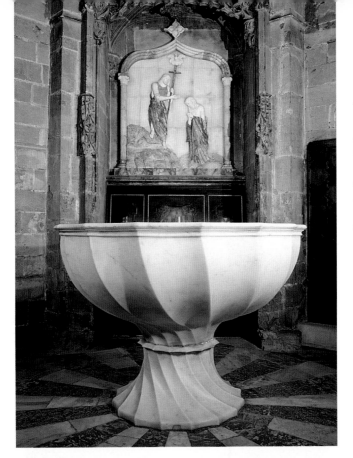

Gothic baptism font in which some historians, with little historic rigour, affirm that the first Indians brought back by Christopher Columbus after his first American voyage of discovery were baptised.

Main doorway (interior). The carving follows a design by the Modernist artist Joan Roig.

We can also see the triforium with the monument used on Holy Thursday and installed in the interior of the Sant Iu Gate.

In the extrados of the entrance arch two medallions representing the Ascension and Pentecost, by the sculptor Antoni Claperós.

Shrine and image of Saint Mark in the baroque Chapel of Sant Marc, by an anonymous artist (1683-1692).

Saint Peter Nolasco received investiture as the first Mercedarian friar at the high altar of the Romanesque Cathedral on 10 August 1281. Baroque altarpiece (1689). Anonymous.

Panel of the Altar of El Roser representing the birth of Jesus, by Agustí Pujol (1705).

Shrine and polychrome image in the Altarpiece of El Roser.

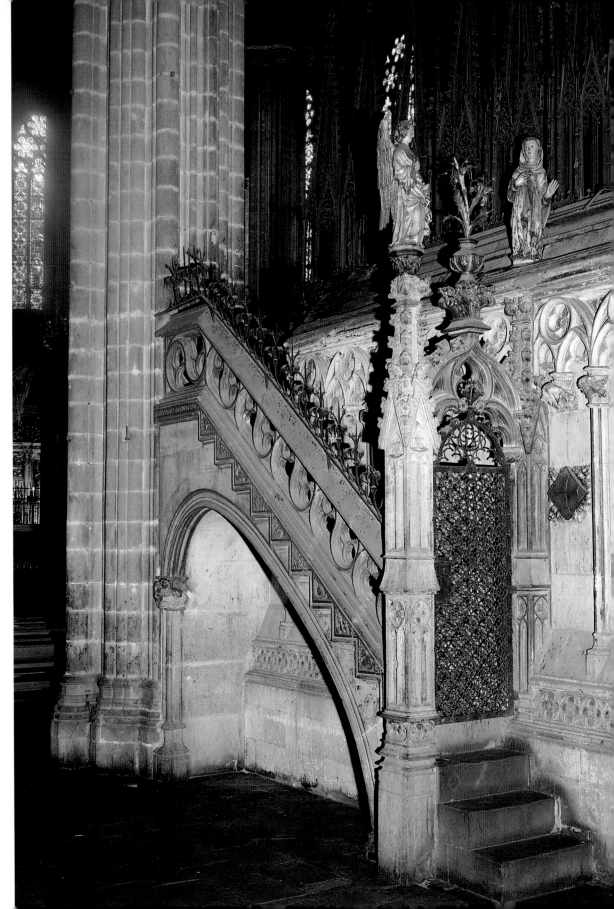

Splendid steps leading up to the throne on the left-hand wall of the choir. The two sculptures (Annunciation) are by the sculptor Jordi Johan (de Déu), though some historians attribute the work to Ça Anglada (1400).

The canonry, or body of canons, was established during the time of Bishop Frodoí in the 9th century. One of the most important elements was the cloister. The present Gothic cloister was built by great architects (such as Escuder) and sculptors (Claperós father and son). The floor contains the burial stones of many families benefactors of the Cathedral (Rocafort, Foix, Cardona, etc) and members of guilds and brotherhoods (tailers, shoemakers, etc).

8. FROM THE CLOISTER AND THE MUSEUM

From the interior of the Cathedral, we enter the cloister through an attractive doorway featuring mid-11th century elements. The capitals are excellent, those on the left figurative and those on the right with floral motifs. When this doorway from the old Romanesque basilica was built, Gothic tympanum and crenellations were added.

The cloister was built during the 14th and 15th centuries, and the wing adjoining the Cathedral during the first decades of the 14th. As can be seen from documents in the diocesan archives and has been demonstrated by recent archaeological investigation, the Romanesque cloister formerly stood in the centre of the present cloister. The Carrer Bisbe wing was built during the bishopric of the patriarch Sapera, the last vault terminated in 1448.

The chapels around the cloister contain various altarpieces transferred here at the start of the present century. The entire cloister is covered with the coats of arms of nobles and brotherhoods: Rocafort, Foix, Castanyer, Cardona, Tresserres, Pla, Nadal Garcés, Joan Andreu Sors, etc. Particularly interesting are the altars of El Sant Crist de Talarn, Sant Josep, Els Màrtirs and La Mare de Déu de la Llum, as well as the tombs of Girona y Sanllehy and the sculptor Josep Llimona. Notable for its decorative value is the frieze crowning the cloister arches. In it are depicted scenes from the Old and New Testaments, as well as the medieval legend of the Tree of the Holy Cross –to which the Cathedral is dedicated–. Some of the gargoyles in the interior are attributed to Claperós.

Also interesting is the *Portal de la Pietat,* a doorway whose tympanum contains a reproduction of the carved wooden sculpture of the Pieta by the German artist Michael Lochner (1490). The original is to be found inside the Cathedral, in the upper gallery.

The interior of the cloister also features a magnificent fountain, the work of the architect Escuder and the sculptors Claperós (father and son). In the centre is a small bronze figure by Emili Colom (1970).

The *Chapel of Santa Llúcia* has a square groundplan and a pointed barrel vault. It was built by Bishop Arnau de Gurb (1284), whose tomb, restored in the last century, was installed in an arcosolium embedded in the left-hand wall. Opposite is another arcosolium, the tomb of Canon Francesc de Santa Coloma, dating to the mid-16th century. This is crowned by a Calvary carved in stone over a background of blue glass. The murals of the altar are by Nuet i Martí (1940-1945). Before this century, this was the Episcopal Chapel of the Holy Virgins. The painting in the tympanum of the doorway is by Joan Llimona (1901).

The Cathedral Museum exhibits many works of great artistic interest, including: Bermejo's *Pieta* (1490), at whose feet is the work's Maecenas, Archdeacon Lluís Desplà; panels painted by Jaume Huguet for the Altarpiece of Sant Bernardí y Sant Miquel; a panel depicting the Virgin Mary surrounded by saints and angel musicians (14th century); a predella of Sant Onofre by Ramon Destorrents; a large painting by Manuel Tramulles (1770), representing Charles III taking possession of the his canonry in the Cathedral; some twills by Pere Serafí, of which we have already spoken; a 15th-century Altarpiece of Tots els Sants; and the baptism font from the Romanesque Cathedral, amongst others.

Some speak poetically of the cloister as the last redoubt of earthly paradise. All in it is magnificent: the view of the belltowers, dome, gargoyles... and a garden with tall palms, magnolias and medlars.

Some of the cloister chapels are of great importance, such as the one containing Talarn's sculpture of Christ crucified.

Statue of the Mare de Déu de la Penya (the Virgin of the Rock), probably another name for the Virgin of Montserrat.

Tombs of the Sanllehy and Girona families, the great Maecenas of the cathedral's main façade.

Chapel of the Mare de Déu de la Llum.

Arnau de Gurb, Bishop of Barcelona, built the chapel now known as of Sant Llúcia (1257-1268). The bishop's mausoleum is on the right, under an arcosolium. Note also the splendid tomb of Francesc de Santa Coloma (14th century).

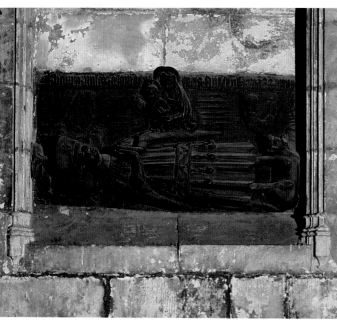

The cloister contains the tomb of a curious personage, half buffoon, half diplomat: Antoni Tallader, also known as Mn. Borra.

Keystone over the cloister fountain, representing Saint George, patron saint of Catalonia.

Beside the cloister fountain is a pool in which geese sport and whose jets amaze visitors, one minute transparent, the next brightly shining.

There are two Saint Georges in the cloister fountain: one in the keystone of the kiosk, by Claperós, the other installed in the waterspout, a magnificent sculpture by the contemporary artist Emili Colom.

There are thirteen geese in the Cathedral cloister, just as there were thirteen in the days of Saint Eulàlia, when she was martyrised during the persecution of Diocletianus in the early-4th century. The geese act as guardians, as they make a great furore at the approach of anyone with doubtful intentions.

The presence of guilds and brotherhoods is a constant throughout the Cathedral, especially in the stones of the cloister, where there are references to the tailors', weavers' and house-builders' guilds.

The feast of Corpus Christi began to be celebrated in Barcelona as soon as Pope John XXII instituted it in the year 1316. The tradition of the «ou com balla» («the egg which dances») is documented as far back as the 18th century, and possible represents the monstrance. Once the procession was over, the choirboys could help themselves to the cherries in the fountain in recompense for their many hours of attendance.

The entrance to the Chapter Museum is through a fine door in the wing of the cloister containing the Chapel of El Santíssim or of El Sant Crist de Lepant. The museum exhibits works of enormous artistic interest. Two of its rooms are particularly important; that known as the Sala de la Capbrevació and the present Chapterhouse, where the canons meet at meetings to designate canonical posts. This 15th-century section also formerly contained the Pia Almoina, or dining room for the poor, until this institution was transferred to what is now the site of the Diocesan Museum (Pla de la Seu no. 7) in Barcelona. The first room, that of la Capbrevació, was where all dominical rights of the lord were settled and recorded, is where visitors are first welcomed to the museum. Here we find the above-mentioned organ twills on display, as well as altarcloths embroidered in the 15th century depicting scenes from the life of Jesus and the Transfiguration, as well as an 11th-century trefoiled font, which predates the font now in use, a Romanesque work with decorative elements going back to Roman times.

In the inner room, precisely in the place where there is a cloistered door, there hangs a large painting of Christ crucified, dating back to 1685 and executed thanks to the munificence of Canon Roig. The frame is by Llàtzer Tramulles (1690) and gilt by Magí Torrebruna in 1691. The present Chapterhouse features the altarpiece by Jaume Huguet dedicated to Saint Bernard and the Guardian Angel, commissioned by the guild of basketmakers and glazers. The work dates back to around 1466.

The museum also contains other altarpieces, such as that of Sant Llorenç (15th century), a 14th-century Gothic panel representing Mary with Baby Jesus, seated on the throne, with, at her feet, angel musicians, a work commissioned by the shoemakers' guild.

In 1970, the statue of Saint Eulàlia, formerly in the tympanum of the door, was installed here. The work is attributed to Claperós father and son.

Also interesting is a large painting portraying Charles III taking possession of the canonry in this very room, by Manuel Tramulles (1770). The upper part of the room is decorated with scenes from the Glorification of Saint Eulàlia and Saint Oleguer (17th century).

However, perhaps the most artistically valuable piece here is the painting of the Pieta (Mary's mourning of Jesus) by the Cordoban artist Bartomeu Bermejo, dating to 1490. This was formerly installed in the Chapel of L'Ardiaca Lluís Desplà, now a tower of the Episcopal Palace housing the Diocesan Archives. The donor (Canon Desplà) is present in the scene depicted. Also featured is Saint Jerome reading a codex in which the word «Montserrat» can be made out.

The barrel vault of the Chapterhouse, which forms part of the Museum, features paintings of two beloved saints: Oleguer and Eulàlia of Barcelona with, in the centre, the Holy Spirit.

The touching, dramatic scene of the Descent from the Cross was magnificently painted by Bartomeu Bermejo in 1490. Oil on wood. The scene is flanked by Saint Jerome and Canon Lluís Desplà i d'Oms (1444-1524).

La Pietat (c. 1490)
de Bartolomé BERMEJO

Bermejo's Pieta is a whole cosmos: the expressions of pain on the face of the Virgin and Jesus are remarkable. The work contains many details, such as a traveller on a white horse.

◁ Saint Jerome reading a codex.

There are many elements represented in Bartolomé Bermejo's painting of the Pieta: cities, clouds, birds flying parallel, animals, flowers...

Butterfly: the head and thorax have to be separated for the head to move. Here, they are not. Butterflies never have pointed wings. The drawing is, therefore, an invention.

Lizard: it is green and the head cannot be seen, but this is, nevertheless, a representation of Lacenta Viridis.

Fly: the head cannot be seen. It could be a bee, Apis Melifica.

Snail: seen perfectly, this is Limnea, with its spiral shell.

Ladybug: clearly not the classical «ladybird». This is a hemiptera, Pyriocoris Apterus

Flowers: the common name for this plant is sow thistle, the scientific name Sonchus Oleraceus. It has the property of calming fevers and thirst. It is grown on riverbanks and in gardens.

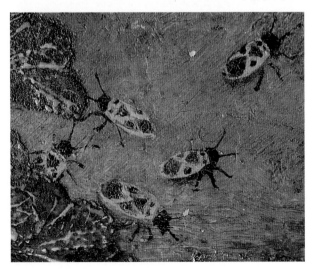

In the prayers of the Rosary we invoke «Sedes sapientae», the seat of wisdom. At this 14th-century table, the Virgin Mary has at her feet angel musicians, and she is flanked by saints.

Embroidered cartoon with representation of the Baptism of Jesus (15th century).

Terra cotta image of Saint Eulàlia, attributed to Claperós (father and son).

Burial of Jesus and other scenes from the predella of the Altarpiece of Sant Bernardí i l'Àngel Custodi, by Jaume Huguet (1462).

Central scenes from the altarpiece by Jaume Huguet, and painting by Manuel Tramulles (1770) depicting Charles III in this very same Chapel and Chapterhouse when he took possession of the canonry.

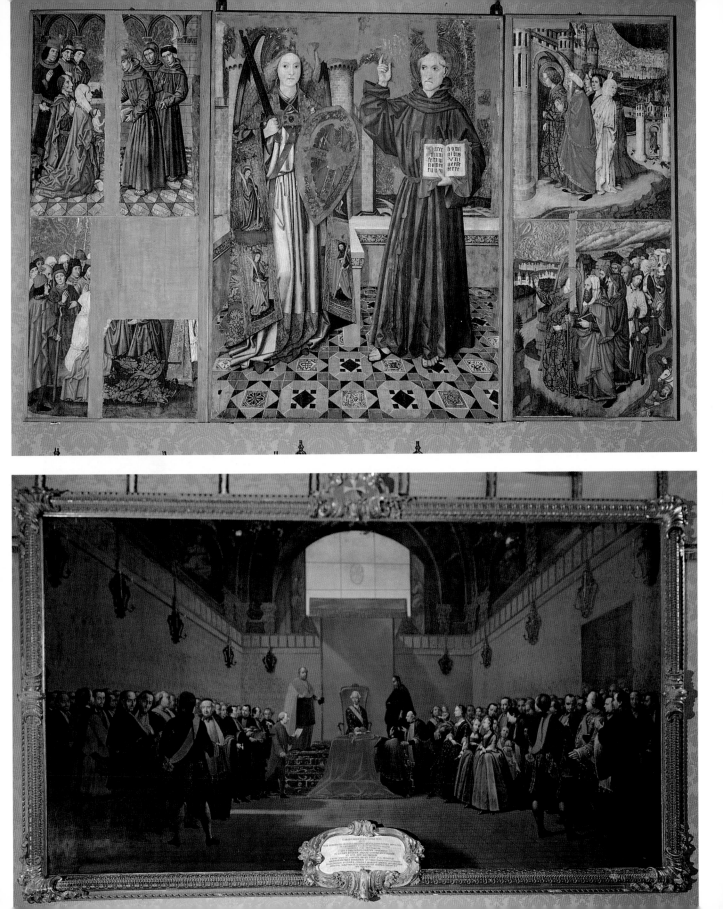

The Cathedral organ was formerly protected by these twills, the work of Pere Serafí, known as Pere de les set pes («Pere of the Seven P's»), due to the saying Pere Pau pinta portes per poc preu («Pere Pau paints doors for a low price»). The work dates to around 1560.

The Cathedral stands in the centre of the city, a gift of God with its arms wide open to all who wish to pray here, to join the Christian assembly or simply to visit it, contemplating the wonders of God in his holy mysteries, its saints and angels who, from on high, protect the city of Barcelona.

Access door to the cloister from Carrer de la Pietat. The relief is attributed to Michael Lochner (1490). The original is now in the triforium; that of the photograph is a reproduction.

Gate of Santa Eulàlia, from Carrer del Bisbe. Flanking the saint, a reproduction, as the original is in the Cathedral Museum, are the coats of arms of the Holy Cross and Bishop Sapera.

Gate of Santa Llúcia, giving access to the chapel of the same name. This chapel predates the Gothic Cathedral and was built by Bishop Arnau de Gurb from 1257 to 1268.

Relief of the Agnus Dei which formed part of a door communicating this chapel with the Episcopal Palace.

As far back as the 11th century it was customary to light candles here to the Holy Cross, Mary, Saint Eulàlia and all the saints traditionally worshipped by the faithful of Barcelona.

FAREWELL

The visit to our Cathedral has reached its end. During the course of this long tour you have made, helped by this guide to the Holy Cathedral Basilica of Barcelona, you have discovered the wealth and complex reality of the first temple in our archdiocese. It is quite possible that the first thing to have attracted your attention was its architectural complexity, which is truly impressive. Next, you will have admired the enormous pictoric and sculptural wealth of the Cathedral, with important Gothic, baroque and Renaissance works. In terms of art, the Cathedral, more than a magnificent museum, is what we might call a treatise on art history. You will also have learned, whilst admiring the nave and aisles and the cloister, much about the history of the city and Catalonia. For this church is the work of generation after generation whose work, art and manner of building a country brought about the construction and enrichment of this authentic marvel you have just visited.

Moreover, the work of an entire people, building and conserving its Cathedral is, above all, a consequence and a manifestation of religious feeling. Faith, translated into the commitment of the believer, creates culture. And it creates culture according to the parameters of idiosyncrasies. Our Cathedral is a clear confession of the faith of the Catalan people which, when expressed, that is, whilst living and saying the Gospel, does so in the Catalan language and in the Catalan manner. This is why the most outstanding characteristic of our Cathedral is its nature of a temple, of a place of religious celebration, of prayer. As you will have noticed during the visit, our Cathedral is not only a temple, it is a living temple. You have come on a tourist and cultural visit, but you will have seen many people in the Cathedral who were there to pray, out of piety or in an act of thanksgiving to God Our Lord for, through the mediation of the Virgin Mary or one of the saints, whose images are venerated here, giving the grace or consolation prayed for. If the example of these people you have seen in the Cathedral has also led you to say a brief prayer, you will have demonstrated your faith and your religious sensitivity, and this spontaneous, joyful gesture of yours during your visit is perhaps the highest possible praise of the pious atmosphere our Cathedral creates and maintains.

The time for goodbyes has come. We thank you with all our heart for your visit. If this guide has been useful to you, we take cheer. If you have found any shortcomings in it, we ask your forgiveness and that you will tell us of them. If we can, we will remedy them so as to improve this publication, which has served you as a guide, in order to make the visit to the Cathedral as pleasant and complete as possible. And if you are pleased with what you have seen and felt during your visit to Barcelona Cathedral, when you reach your homes, please spread the news about the visit to our temple amongst any friends or family who plan to come to Barcelona.

As we say at the end of our services, we also say to you now, Go in peace. And may the peace, joy and the light of Jesus Christ Our Lord always be with you.

Josep. M. Aragonès Rebollar
Canon «Fabriquer» of Barcelona Cathedral.

BIBLIOGRAPHY

AINAUD, J.; GUDIOL, J.; VERRIÉ, F. P. *Catálogo Monumental de España. La ciudad de Barcelona.* (Madrid, 1947).

ALCOLEA, S.: *La pintura en Barcelona durante el siglo XVIII.* «Anales y Boletín de los Museos de Arte de Barcelona», vol. XV, 1961-1962. Barral

BASSEGODA NONELL, J.: *Bóvedas medievales a la romana.* Memorias de la Real Academia de Ciencias y Artes de Barcelona, vol. XLIII, núm. 8 (287-382).

BASSEGODA NONELL, J.: *Coneguem la Catedral de Barcelona,* 1996.

CARRERAS CANDI, F.: *Les obres de la catedral de Barcelona,* «Boletín de la Academia de Buenas Letras» vol. VIII, años CLXXXV-CLXXXVI, 22, 128, 302 i 575. (Barcelona 1913-1914).

CIRICI, A. I GUMÍ, J.: *L'Art Gòtic Català. Segles XIII i XIV.* Ed. 62. Barcelona 1977.

CIRICI, A. I GUMÍ, J.: *L'Art Gòtic Català. Segles XV i XVI.* Ed. 62. Barcelona 1979.

CIRICI, A. I GUMÍ, J.: *Arquitectura gótica catalana.* Ed. Lumen. Barcelona, 1968.

CUBELES, A.: *Anotacions sobre la producció historiogràfica a propòsit de la catedral de Barcelona en el període 1882-1952.* revista «d'Art» 19 (1913). pàgs. 15-28.

DALMASES, N.: *L'orfebreria.* Col. Conèixer Catalunya. Dopesa, 2. Barcelona, 1979.

DURAN I SANPERE, A.: *Itinerarios artísticos: la Catedral de Barcelona.* Ed. Aymà, S.L. Barcelona, 1952.

FÀBREGA I GRAU, A.: *La Catedral de Barcelona.* Guia turística, Barcelona, Ed. Balmes, 1969.

LIAÑO MARTÍNEZ, E.: *La Catedral de Barcelona.* (León, 1984)

MARTÍ BONET, J.M.-NIQUI PUIGVERT, L.- MIQUEL MASCORT, F.: Ponç de Gualba. Roma, 1989.

MAS, J.: *Guía itinerario de la catedral de Barcelona.* Imprenta la Renaixensa. Barcelona, 1916.

TERÉS TOMÁS, M.R. *Pere Ça Anglada, maestro del coro de la catedral de Barcelona: Aspectos documentales y formales.* Revista d'Art. Departament d'Art de la Universitat de Barcelona, núm. 5. Barcelona, 1979.

VERRIÉ, F.P.: *El arquitecto Bernat Roca y sus obras barcelonesas.* Diputación histórica, VIII. Barcelona, 199.

VERRIÉ, F.P.: FLORENSA, A; DURAN I SANPERE, A. L'art gòtic, en l'Art Català. vol. I. Ed. Aymà. Barcelona, 1955.

1. Cathedral front
2. Pia Almoina
3. Main Entrance
4. Dome
5. Chapel of the Immaculada Concepció
6. Chapel of El Santíssim Sacrament, El Sant Crist de Lepant i Sant Olegari
7. Chapel of Sant Antoni de Padua, Confressor; Sants Cosme i Damià
8. Chapel of Sant Josep Oriol
9. Chapel of Sant Pancraç i Sant Roc
10. Chapel of Sant Raimond de Penyafort
11. Chapel of Sant Sant Pau, San Caeità, Santo Domingo de Guzmán, Sant Pere, Santa Cecilia i Santa Marta.
12. Chapel of Nostra Senyora del Pilar
13. Chapel of Sant San Pacià i Sant Francesc Xavier
14. *Trascoro* (frontispiece of the choir)
15. Interior of the choir
16. Baptistery
17. Chapel of Sant Sant Sever, Bishop of Barcelona
18. Chapel of Sant Marc
19. Chapel of Sant Bernadí de Siena
20. Chapel of Nostra Senyora del Rosari
21. Chapel of Santa Maria Magdalena, Sant Bartolomeu i Santa Isabel.
22. Chapel of L'Immaculat Cor de Maria, Sant Sebastià i Santa Tecla
23. Chapel of Nostra Senyora de l'Al.legria; Sant Pío X
24-25. Chapel of Nostra Senyora de Montserrat.
26. Access to terraces (lift)
27. Door of Sant Iu
28. Presbytery
29. Crypt of Santa Eulàlia
30. Chapel of Les Ànimes del Purgatori
31. Chapel of El Sagrat Cor de Jesus
32. Chapel of Nostra Senyora de la Mercè
33. Chapel of «Sants Llocs de Terra Santa» (Sant Sepulcre)
34. Chapel of Sant Pere, Apóstol; Sant Martí y Sant Ambrosi, Bisbes
35. Chapel of Santa Elena
36. Chapel of Sant Joan Baptista i Sant Josep
37. Chapel of Sant Beneit
38. Chapel of La Visitació de Nostra Senyora, Verge de Fàtima; Sant Lucas i Sant Sebastià
39. Chapel of Nostra Senyora del Carme, Sant Antoni Abat i Sant Frances d'Assis
40. Sacristy
41. The cathedral's artistic treasure
42. Tomb of the Counts of Barcelona
43. Cloister
44. Door of La Pietat
45. Cloister fountain
46. Cathedral museum
47. Door of Santa Eulàlia
48. Chapter Archives
49. Chapel of Santa Llúcia
50. Shop.

© Editorial Escudo de Oro, S.A.
I.S.B.N. 84-378-1813-3
Printed by FISA - Editorial Escudo de Oro, S.A.
Palaudarias, 26 - 08004 - Barcelona
Dep. Legal B. 29817-2000
www.eoro.com
e-mail: editorial@eoro.com

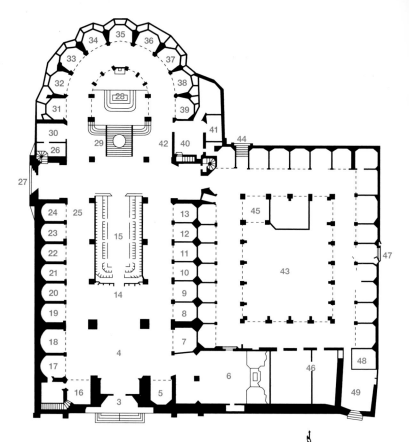